P9-DDW-104

Hair-Care Millionaire

Madam C. J. Walker and Her Amazing Business

Edwin Brit Wyckoff

Enslow Elementary

an imprint of

Enslow Publishers, Inc.

40 Industrial Road
Box 398
Berkeley Heights, NJ 07922
USA

http://www.enslow.com

Content Adviser

A'Lelia Bundles

Great-great-granddaughter and biographer of Madam C. J. Walker

Series Literary Consultant

Allan A. De Fina, PhD

Dean, College of Education and Professor of Literacy Education

New Jersey City University

Past President of the New Jersey Reading Association

Enslow Elementary, an imprint of Enslow Publishers, Inc.

Enslow Elementary® is a registered trademark of Enslow Publishers, Inc.

Library of Congress Cataloging-in-Publication Data

Wyckoff, Edwin Brit.
  Hair-care millionaire : Madam C. J. Walker and her amazing business / Edwin Brit Wyckoff.
      p. cm. — (Genius at work! Great inventor biographies)
  Includes bibliographical references and index.
  Summary: "Read about the life of Madam C.J. Walker, and find out how she created a hair care empire, and helped African Americans in the early 1900s"—Provided by publisher.
  ISBN 978-0-7660-3449-5
  1. Walker, C. J., Madam, 1867-1919—Juvenile literature. 2. African American women executives—Biography—Juvenile literature. 3. Cosmetics industry—United States—History—Juvenile literature. 4. Women millionaires—United States—Biography—Juvenile literature. I. Title.
  HD9970.5.C672W3588 2011
  338.7'66855—dc22
  [B]
                                            2009043014

Printed in the United States of America

052010 Lake Book Manufacturing, Inc., Melrose Park, IL

10 9 8 7 6 5 4 3 2 1

To Our Readers
We have done our best to make sure all Internet addresses in this book were active and appropriate when we went to press. However, the author and the publisher have no control over and assume no liability for the material available on those Internet sites or on other Web sites they may link to. Any comments or suggestions can be sent by e-mail to comments@enslow.com or to the address on the back cover.

Every effort has been made to locate all copyright holders of material used in this book. If any errors or omissions have occurred, corrections will be made in future editions of this book.

♻ Enslow Publishers, Inc., is committed to printing our books on recycled paper. The paper in every book contains 10% to 30% post-consumer waste (PCW). The cover board on the outside of each book contains 100% PCW. Our goal is to do our part to help young people and the environment too!

Illustration Credits: Artville LLC, p. 8; Property of Black Legacy Images; Dawn Spears, President., pp. 1 (upper left), 6; Enslow Publishers, Inc., pp. 9 (bottom), 12, 15 (top); Madam C. J. Walker Collection, Courtesy of the Indiana Historical Society, pp. 1 (lower right), 4, 9 (top), 11, 14, 15 (bottom), 16, 17, 19, 21, 22, 27; Library of Congress, pp. 18, 24; National Guard Image Gallery, p. 25; National Park Service, p. 28; Shutterstock, pp. 3, 10, 13.

Cover Illustrations: front cover—courtesy of the Indiana Historical Society (portrait); property of Black Legacy Images, Dawn Spears, President (can); back cover—Shutterstock.

Contents

Madam C. J. Walker

Chapter 1

Knock, Knock—Who's There?

Way back in the early 1900s, a determined woman earned a huge fortune—and it all started with the sound of knuckles knocking on doors. When people answered, they saw a thirty-four-year-old African-American woman standing there. It was Sarah McWilliams—soon to become famous as Madam C. J. Walker.

She began to talk softly and eagerly as she held out a small tin of "Wonderful Hair Grower" ointment she had invented. It could make a black woman's head of hair grow longer and thicker, she said. It could also make hair wonderfully easy to style. She treated women's scalps herself and showed them how to style

Madam C. J. Walker invented a whole line of beauty products for African-American women.

their hair. She also taught her customers how to eat right and be healthy.

She taught some women to walk out on low-paying jobs. Then she trained them to sell her amazing hair-growing ointment. Later on she gave some of them courage to open hair salons—along with the pride to take charge of their family's lives.

That little tin of ointment was the first in a line of beauty products she invented. Like a whirlwind, she traveled from city to city, building a network of thousands of sales agents.

Madam C. J. Walker went from being a single mother in a dead-end job to being the richest African-American woman in the United States. And she became a celebrity the way Oprah Winfrey is today. It all started with the sound of knuckles knocking on doors.

Chapter 2

Making Changes

Sarah was born to Owen and Minerva Breedlove in tiny Delta, Louisiana, in 1867. Both her parents died from terrible fevers no one could control. Sarah had the shock of becoming an orphan at age seven. She was taken in by her sister, who lived in Vicksburg, Mississippi, and who was married to a very nasty

man. Sarah escaped by marrying Moses McWilliams when she was fourteen. It was "in order to get a home of my own," she later said. Lelia, her only child, was born

The cabin on a Louisiana plantation where Sarah was born.

when Sarah was seventeen. Without warning, her world was torn apart again when her husband died suddenly. She was twenty and all alone.

The young mother moved up along the Mississippi River to St. Louis, Missouri. To support herself and her child, she worked hours every day washing laundry in boiling water, earning less than a dollar

and fifty cents a day. She married John Davis in 1894. He turned out to be a mean and fussy man who did not believe in doing much work himself. They divorced after nine bad years. Something had to change.

Sarah peered at herself in a mirror. She hated her hair. Like many women of that time, she washed her hair only once a week, and she used harsh chemicals to make it easier to style. As a result, it was short and brittle and broken at the ends. There were bare spots where it would not even grow. Then she took a good hard look at her whole life and realized that she had to work on herself.

The thirty-three-year-old laundry worker decided to sign up for night school. She had to learn to read and write. She also practiced thinking things

These photos show Sarah before and after using her "Wonderful Hair Grower."

out carefully and speaking out clearly. As poor as she was, she began to sound like the successful businesswoman she would become one day.

In 1902, her confident voice impressed Annie Minerva Pope-Turnbo, who ran a business selling hairdressing products. Sarah became one of her sales agents. She sold Turnbo's products day after day, then plunged her arms into hot, heavy laundry night after night. As hard as she worked, Sarah never had

Sarah began selling hairdressing products door to door.

much money. In 1905 she packed a supply of Turnbo's hair creams and moved out west to try Denver, Colorado. She had a handful of dollars in her pocket, and nothing more.

12

Chapter 3

Starting Over Again

As Madam C. J. Walker told it, one night a voice in her dreams spoke to her. A man dressed in African robes gave her his ancient formula for growing beautiful black hair. He whispered secret ingredients one by one, night after night, for three nights. There were beeswax and copper sulfate, sulfur and violet perfume, and secret things from Africa. Some people said that a chemist had helped her. But Sarah could never be shaken from her memory of the magical, mysterious man in her dreams.

Inventing the special product.

Packaging it attractively.

Distributing it through sales agents.

Training agents to make them experts on health and beauty.

Spending money on advertising, using photographs of Madam C. J. Walker.

Getting free publicity stories about Walker into newspapers so people knew her and trusted her.

Running promotions such as free hair treatments to bring in new customers.

Sarah said that some of the supplies for the recipe came from Africa. She mixed batches of her "Wonderful Hair Grower" carefully in a laboratory hidden in a tiny attic. And she went out knocking on doors with her own invention in hand. She was driven by excitement and ambition. And she was unstoppable.

In 1906, Sarah married once more. She had met Charles Joseph Walker back in St. Louis. He followed her to Denver, where she became Madam C. J. Walker. They loved working up ideas to build what people today call a "hot brand."

A demonstration of how to comb hair

15

The company earned $3,672 in 1907. A business panic battered the whole country in 1908. Many businesses collapsed. The unsinkable Madam Walker kept on pushing sales. In that awful year she dared to open Lelia College in Pittsburgh, Pennsylvania, which taught hairstyling. The business surged ahead, earning $8,782 in 1908, which was big money back then. Earnings doubled, and then doubled again and again. Then they went up to hundreds of thousands of dollars a year.

Students at Lelia College, a school Madam Walker opened to teach people how to become hair stylists

Walker and her husband drifted apart and divorced in 1912. She was left with one valuable thing: She kept the name Madam C. J. Walker.

Earnings soared to almost five hundred thousand dollars a year by 1917. Walker had bought property in the Midwest. She built a huge factory in Indianapolis, Indiana, which had its own movie theater. She bought luxurious houses in Los Angeles and New York City. She helped her daughter, Lelia (who later changed her name to A'Lelia), open a

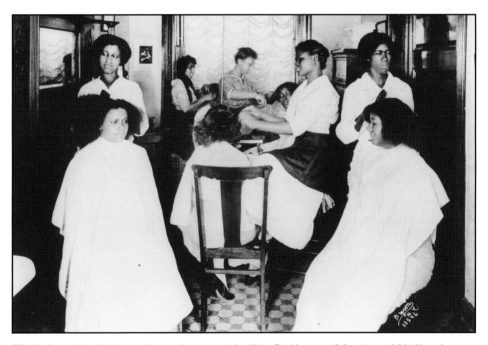

This is a hairdressing class at Lelia College. Madam Walker's daughter, Lelia, is seated at left. Lelia's adopted daughter, Mae, is standing at back in braids.

glamorous beauty salon in Harlem. And she built a thirty-room mansion on the Hudson River north of New York City, naming it Villa Lewaro.

A man in uniform drove her seven-passenger touring car. Even more, she enjoyed driving herself in a two-passenger electric car downtown to Tiffany, the famous jewelry store, then zipping back to one of her

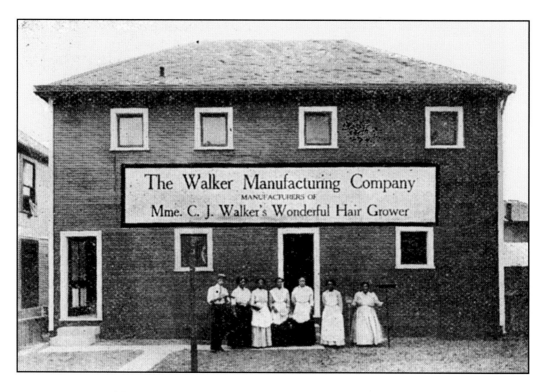

Madam Walker's first factory, in Indianapolis

Madam Walker enjoyed driving in this two-passenger car.

homes for big parties with poets, politicians, and opera stars.

Women's clubs begged Walker to come talk to them. She had stunned the public by giving a thousand dollars to help build an African-American YMCA in Indianapolis. Her success opened doors for African Americans and for all women. But one very special door was closed in her face.

Chapter 4

The War to Win Over Washington

Booker T. Washington was the most respected African-American man in the United States. He headed the Tuskegee Institute in Alabama, a famous college teaching African Americans.

Walker wanted to be a speaker at his National Negro Business League. But Washington would not invite her. He had no respect for hairstyling. She insisted that her agents were taught how to grow and style hair, not to straighten it.

Walker raced down to Tuskegee and knocked on Washington's door. She said, "I want them to know that I am in the business world, not for myself alone, but to do all the good I can do for the uplift of my race." He said she could speak to a very small group, but that was all.

Madam Walker, photographed with Booker T. Washington (on her left) and other black leaders

At the big National Negro Business League meeting a few months later, Walker rose to her feet. She said, "I went into a business that is despised . . . the business of growing hair. I have proven beyond the question of a doubt that I do grow hair." Booker T. Washington tried to stop her. But she would not be silenced.

> I am a woman who came from the cotton fields of the South. From there I was promoted to the washtub. From there I was promoted to the cook kitchen. And from there I promoted myself into the business of manufacturing hair goods and preparations. I have built my own factory on my own ground.

21

A Real Opportunity for Women who wish to become Independent.

MmeWALKER'S SYSTEM

of Scientific Scalp Treatment and Sales of her Hair Preparations are giving support to more than 100,000 people in this Industry. Come in and learn how.

Madam C. J. Walker offered opportunities for African-American women to support themselves.

The crowd of quiet men began to come alive with enthusiasm. She raised her voice. "Please don't applaud. Let me talk." The next year Booker T. Washington gave in. Madam Walker spoke from the big stage at the business league.

Next Madam C. J. Walker confronted another Washington. This time it was a city rather than a person—Washington, D.C., capital of the United States. In 1917 there had been a wave of lynchings—murders of African-American citizens. She and others demanded that President Woodrow Wilson speak out against the crimes. He said nothing. In protest, ten thousand African Americans marched in a courageous, silent parade down Fifth Avenue in New York. Another twenty thousand watched in silence. There was only the hollow beat of drums turning the day into a vast funeral service.

In 1919, a deeply angered Walker was among several African Americans who demanded better

To protest violence against African Americans, ten thousand people marched through the streets of New York.

treatment of the black soldiers who had fought in Europe in World War I. President Wilson had a slogan: "Make the world safe for democracy." Madam Walker roared back, "Make America safe for *all* Americans."

The Harlem Hellfighters in battle

The all-black 369th regiment, known as the Harlem Hellfighters, came home wearing medals for bravery that France had given each member of the unit—but the United States gave them nothing. The woman who had been a fighter all her life honored them with all her heart and soul.

Chapter 5

Living the Plan

In less than fifteen years, the laundry worker with brittle, thinning hair had built a corporation earning what would be millions of dollars today. She raised a daughter who became a celebrity herself. Lelia adopted a teenager, Mae Bryant, who grew up to hold important jobs in the business. Madam C. J. Walker loved being a grandmother and something of a godmother to her workers.

She could have opened Walker hair salons everywhere, but said, "It is better to let [women] work up their own business." So she loaned money to women so they could gamble on themselves. She even set up a union for her workers when many businesspeople feared that unions would have too much power.

Women at the cosmetics counter at the Madam C. J. Walker Beauty Shoppe. Though Walker could have had many more salons, she encouraged women to open their own businesses.

The constant pressure of work began to wear her out. Doctors warned her to stop. She rested a short time, then plunged back into the work of building her brand. Long ago, the heavy work in the cotton fields and the laundry tub had set the driving rhythm of her whole life.

Now she wore lovely, soft silks, and she lived in beautiful places she had paid for herself. Her mind was lively with new business ideas, but her body began to give out. "I am not going to die, because I have so much work to do yet," she said quietly. "I want to live to help my race." Death came Sunday

Villa Lewaro, Walker's home on the Hudson River

morning, May 25, 1919. Newspaper headlines flashed across much of the world. Madam C. J. Walker was only fifty-one.

The legend was gone. The business went on for five more decades. Her message that women could learn and earn and control their own destinies is alive today. She believed in planning her life and living the plan with all her might. This determined lady once said: "I had to make my own living and my own opportunity. But I made it! Don't sit down and wait for the opportunities to come. Get up and make them." She always did.

Timeline

1867 Sarah Breedlove born December 23.

1875 Both parents die, leaving Sarah an orphan.

1882 Marries Moses McWilliams, who dies five years later.

1885 Daughter, Lelia, born in Delta, Louisiana.

1894 Marries John Davis in St. Louis, Missouri; divorces him after nine years.

1903 Works as saleslady in St. Louis.

1906 Marries C. J. Walker after moving to Denver, Colorado. Sets up Madam C. J. Walker hair-growing business.

1908 Moves operations to Pittsburgh, Pennsylvania. Starts Lelia College to teach hairdressing.

1910 Builds factory in Indianapolis, Indiana, as sales grow.

1912 Makes major speech at National Negro Business League convention.

1917 Calls on President Woodrow Wilson to speak out against lynching.

1919 Honors African-American war heroes.

1919 Dies on May 25, at her mansion on New York's Hudson River.

Words to Know

formula—A list of chemicals or other things in a product.

ingredient—One item in a formula or recipe.

league—A group of people who work or play together.

legend—A story about a celebrated person, or a person about whom many stories are told.

lynching—Murder committed by a mob of people.

ointment—A soft, oily substance used to heal, soften, or protect the skin or hair.

union—A group of workers who join together to fight for their rights to fair wages and working conditions.

Books

Braun, Sandra. *Incredible Women Inventors*. Toronto: Second Story Press, 2007.

Bundles, A'lelia. *Madam C. J. Walker*. New York: Chelsea House, 2008.

Stille, Darlene R. *Madam C. J. Walker: Entrepreneur and Millionaire*. Minneapolis: Compass Point Books, 2007.

Internet Addresses

The Black Inventor Online Museum: Madam C. J. Walker
<http://www.blackinventor.com/pages/madamewalker.html>

Indiana's Popular History: Madam C. J. Walker
<http://www.indianahistory.org/pop_hist/people/walker.html>

Madam C. J. Walker Official Site
<http://www.madamcjwalker.com/>

Index